D1178023

TEACHING THE EUCHARIST

Teaching the Eucharist

by
Joseph Yperman

Translated by
M. D. Leitch

PAULIST PRESS DEUS BOOKS

NEW YORK   GLEN ROCK   TORONTO
AMSTERDAM   LONDON

Contents

Foreword

The eucharist, the breaking of bread, is a sign which is not "self-evident" to us; it has its roots in a culture other than our own, and consequently we do not feel our way into it spontaneously. Yet it has certain points in common with our modern feeling for life.

Proceeding from a discussion of the *activity of signs* and of *thankful remembrance,* I shall try to clarify somewhat the content, ground structure and scope of the celebration of the eucharist. Since various attempts are now being made to make the liturgy more adaptable, I should like to contribute something toward a better understanding of the sign-activity peculiar to the eucharist itself. I intend to formulate a master catechesis, putting forward an interpretation which will attempt to explain what this is actually all about.

In a following publication, which will deal with the task confronting the Church in the world, and what the liturgical gathering should signify as an assembly of the local church, I hope to open up several further perspectives to extend the scope of a liturgy that is closer to life, and to broaden the range of responsible liturgical parish work.

I am opening this present study with a hymn by H. Oosterhuis. The book as a whole could even be considered a commentary on this hymn.

I am also pleased to use this hymn as a starting point for the sake of the writer himself, since H. Oosterhuis is, in my opinion, one of the few who have made, up to the present, an original contribution to the renovation of the liturgy in the Dutch language.

J.Y.

Louvain, June 15, 1966

Let Us Thankfully Remember

Let us thankfully remember the acts of the Lord,
His life, his death, and his rising;
And sincerely be converted to Jesus,
Our God and our guide through life.

How should we ever have known the way,
If Jesus had not followed it to the end?
Who would we be, if he had not come
To endure our death with his body?

How could we ever have lived for each other,
If he had not shown us what love is,
He who abandoned himself even to death,
He, Son of God, humbly serving us all.

H. OOSTERHUIS

1

The World of Signs

A sign is a wonderful thing. Through signs we come to life and through signs we speak with each other. By speaking to each other in signs, life unfolds and history is made.

The world of signs is a world of wonders. If we cannot interpret the signs, or if we cannot use them, our life does not develop fully. If we are not familiar with the world of signs, we lose contact with our innermost selves, with one another and with God.

THROUGH SIGNS WE COME TO LIFE

Life comes into existence and acquires its human form by means of signs. The spirit and the flesh, the inner being and the sign—these do not exist separated from each other. A separate inner life, as such, does not exist in mankind. Man has his human inner life and his intimate thoughts, yet these are not separated from external conduct; on the contrary, these acquire thereby their human form and their living development. Man only comes to life in signs. The sign is epiphany: the appearance and manifestation of the person. Man's innermost self leads a visible existence. We exist in signs, and without signs we do not exist. Anyone who has ever contemplated the relationship between thinking and doing, or between thought and conduct, or the relationship between thinking and speaking, or between thought and word, will have little difficulty understanding these assertions. For he knows that thought has its embodiment in human behavior and in the word.

The most primary form of thinking is expressed in man's intelligent behavior. It is more primitive and original than thought transformed into words.

Professor Kwant, in his book *Wijsbegeerte van de ontmoeting*,[1] makes a fine analogy in this connection, which he illustrates with the example of the soccer player who chooses his position, intercepts the ball, considers the situation on the field and then passes the ball on in an intelligent fashion. This player "knows" more, and knows

[1] R. C. Kwant, *Wijsbegeerte van de ontmoeting,* pp. 31-33.

it better, with his legs, head and eyes, than he knows it in theory. If he has to teach someone else how to intercept a ball, he will be more likely to do this by demonstrating it than by explaining it theoretically. There is thus a real knowing through the body. He also adds to this that it would be erroneous to assume that this thinking precedes the action, giving the action merely the function of executing it. The intelligent action itself is the embodiment of a spontaneous thought-process: this is effected in the action itself and there it becomes flesh and blood. "Thought exists *in the behavior itself*."

The most perfect form of thinking is expressed verbally. The word is the body of the completed thought. The thought does not exist within our brain as a finished product which must then be communicated by means of the word. No, for the thought itself comes into being only in the word and in the finding of the word. It is in the word that the sense is completed. Understanding can only be fully developed in verbalization.

Sometimes while reading a book, or when studying, I suddenly gain an insight that makes me think I have seen something. This is a "sight which precedes articulation and from which speech is born." [2] But then I realize that I must first put what I see into words in order to gain full insight into it, and also in order to be able to judge

[2] *Ibid.*, p. 56.

whether I have observed well. In searching for the word,
the thought is actually searching for itself.[3]

To believe that the completed thought has an independent existence outside the word is an illusion. It is
true that a thought, once completed in the word, can become a potential possession; and I can even become, as
it were, fused with it. Nevertheless, I cannot manage to
call this thought to life again without the word. Often I
have trouble finding words to express an earlier thought,
and must search again for my words. I then become
aware of the fact that the search for the words which I
need in order to re-express what I have already seen, is
again a search for the thought itself. Through finding my
words, the right words, I again catch hold of the thought.
This indicates once more that thought and word are
completely interwoven with one another. Saying and
understanding do not exist separately. The real word is
simply a verbalized thought, and the completed thought
is nothing more than a thought-out word. My thoughts
gain existence in my words, and without words they cannot achieve full existence. In speaking I gain insight and
my human existence expands. Man lives in the word he
pronounces; he is this word. Thus it becomes clearer that,
to a person brought up on the Bible, a divine word is not
merely a word of God (in the sense that it is a word origi-

[3] Cf. Merleau-Ponty, *Phénomenologie de la perception,* p. 206, and
also Kwant, *op. cit.* pp. 54-59.

nating from God), but God himself is speaking in our midst: in his word he is articulately present among us.

The word is not simply an external reference to the thought; the thought iself comes to life in the word. We should not know another person's thought through his word, if it were not embodied in it.[4]

What holds true for the relationship between conduct and thought, and for the relationship between word and thought, is true of all signs: reality is present in the signs themselves, without signs no reality and no life exist for man.

It is also wrong to regard the sign merely as a reference: as something visible which refers to an invisible content, to an idea, to a feeling, or to one of life's values. A sign is far more, and quite different from a reference to reality. Reality, life and the person come into being in the sign and gain further development. We may then also say that the sign is reality itself, in the sense that reality actually exists within the sign; this, however, does not mean that one particular sign covers all reality.

A line is often drawn between sign and significance. This consequently fails to consider that the sign is the embodiment of life itself, that the sign is reality itself in a reincarnated form, that is, in man's form of existence and in man's conception of reality. One is still inclined to think of man as being made up of an eternal soul, ex-

---

[4] See Kwant, *op. cit.,* 58.

isting independently, and of a transitory mortal body. We have long enough been subjected to all sorts of dualistic philosophies that still have an enormous influence on our views of mankind. If the philosophy of natural thinking drifts so easily into dualism, and if this natural thinking is so readily inclined to separate sign from significance, this does not mean that these really are separated, but, paradoxically enough, that a reality actually is embodied in the sign. The reality-content of the genuine sign makes it actually possible to believe that it must be an entity in itself, and that it can have its own independent existence, exclusive of the person who provides the significance.

Body and soul do not exist in themselves as two conjoined realities. In the physical form only the one man exists. The great and multiform physical being is the primary sign in which man comes to life and through which he achieves his development.

THE COMMUNITY COMES INTO EXISTENCE THROUGH SIGNS

The physical form is the first great sign through which we appear to each other. In the signs our existence for each other is revealed. The relationship between people comes into being in signs, and through signs it is further developed.

Thus, for example, relationship is expressed in a kiss. The relationship comes into existence in the kiss, and thereby gains further development. Through this sign, the relationship comes to life; the sign is the relationship itself. With the kiss I not only indicate that I am fond of the other person, but in the kiss I myself become dear to the other person: the kiss is love itself, embodied in a sign.

A sign is therefore much more than an indication of the relationship. Nor is it a signal that proclaims something else: smoke means fire; a red light indicates danger. But a signal is still not a sign. No relationship lives within it. The sign does not *point to* a reality outside itself; it is permeated with reality—with its own reality. Reality penetrates it, whereas the signal is merely concerned with pointing out. A sign can, of course, be relegated to the function of a signal. Judas caused a sign to become degraded to a signal: "Whomsoever I shall kiss . . . hold him fast." [5] Jesus answers him: "Judas, betrayest thou the Son of man with a kiss?" [6]

Signs are not used to point something out, but to bring a relationship to life, to establish a contact, to make a personal appeal. A signal must have only one meaning. A sign must be expressive. It must summon reality and

[5] Matthew 26, 48.
[6] Luke 22, 48.

make it present. It must be a suggestive expression of an abundant reality which defies formulation and is too great for words.

Only through signs do we come to exist with and for one another. The relationship, in its search for signs, is searching for itself. No love exists that assumes no signs. A relationship can, of course, live on through signs from the past, at least for a time; but as time passes, the existence of the relationship is threatened.

ACTIVITY OF SIGNS

A sign is never static. A sign is always involved with an action: with a person's action, or with an action that calls to life a relationship between two persons. We can express it best by speaking of sign-*activity*. Word and kiss are really abstractions; actually we are dealing with speaking and kissing.

OBJECTS MADE SUBJECTIVE TO SIGNS

Frequently we include in our sign-activity objects that already exist. When, for instance, a gift is given, an already existing object is absorbed into the structure of the sign-activity and into the structure of the giving.

Imagine, for example, that I have not forgotten my mother's birthday, but that I avail myself of the occasion to express my esteem for her by giving her a box of chocolates. When I buy these chocolates as a gift for my mother, they become something more than they were when they still lay in the shop window. They have become absorbed into the framework of a new human sign-activity. They become much more than they ever had the power to be in themselves. They become a personal gift. I am giving much more than something material, for with this gift I am expressing my relationship to my mother. I am giving an actual form to my esteem, and my mother receives the proof of it. Through this gift, I exist in a new way for my mother; my esteem assumes tangible form. Naturally, I am not physically or spatially present in my gift, but I am indeed personally present. I call to life my personal attitude toward my mother. I am not there physically, yet I am there in reality; I am there with my attentiveness and my gratitude, with my devotion and my love, with my better self.

Within the framework of gift-giving, it is the gift that is important. I did not buy just anything. I bought really fine chocolates. I wish to give proof of the quality of my relationship through the quality of the chocolates. The object included within the sign-activity thus clarifies the quality of the sign-activity as a whole. I consider my relationship to my mother important. I have been willing to spend money on it. I have bought a good gift, and this wholly characterizes my relationship.

If the object-as-such, having become absorbed by the sign-activity, contributes to the sign-value of this whole activity on the one hand, it becomes, on the other hand, related to it in a particular way (that is, through being placed in relation to the whole of the sign-activity), and it is, as it were, re-modelled. Through being absorbed into the new context of gift-giving, it becomes permeated by this sign-activity's own meaning. The chocolates remain completely chocolates, yet they also become completely my gift. The most essential thing is that they now signify my relationship; my relationship is represented in them; I give evidence of my esteem through them. The two characteristics of being fine chocolates, and of being my gift do not exclude, but rather complement each other.[7] A sign-activity of this kind always reveals this reciprocal supplementation. To interpret the value of a sign correctly, it is important always to see an object within the framework of the sign-activity with which it has become identified. If we isolate it and make it independent of this, we can easily drift into the world of magic: we then regard it as something charged with strength, no longer as the embodiment of a personal claim.

When I take into my sign-activity an object outside myself, in order to address myself personally to someone else, then I do this because my own physical equip-

---

[7] This sign-activity could also be called symbol-activity, since two realities, two meanings, are brought together (sym-ballein) in it. But we have refrained from using this word because we are aware that this word—unfortunately—is usually misunderstood, viz. in the sense of: "it is only symbolical, not actually real."

ment is in some way deficient as a sign. I say it with flowers because my words are insufficient. I summon forth my best culinary arts in order that a meal may profusely and irreplaceably express my festive mood, and absorb others into it. The object which is absorbed into the sign-activity becomes subjective to it, an extension of one's own physical being. It becomes a token of my personal attunement and is integrated in it.

Whenever an object becomes subjective to a sign, this also presents new possibilities as an extension of the human physical state. The gift possesses the possibility of maintaining within itself a personal representation (a personal appeal), even when the donor is not present.

VERACITY AND SIGN-VALUE

If we stated with apparent naïveté in the foregoing paragraphs that life comes into being through the sign, so that we can say the sign is the embodiment of life itself, and if we also claimed that our relationship with our fellow men is brought to life through the sign, so that we can say that the sign is the embodiment of the relationship itself, this has possibly given rise to a certain feeling of uneasiness; and rightly so.

We have illustrated that this can be so, and we also have the feeling that it should be so. There is, nevertheless, another possibility: the sign can also be a lie. Its existence is constantly threatened by falsity. This is caused by the basic ambiguity of the human being. This two-sidedness has its most radical form in our freedom. Truthfulness is a task for man: veracity in existence and in coexistence. We can verify signs according to the degree in which we succeed in this assignment of truthfulness. Only when we are truthful in our signs do they acquire their real sign-value and really become signs. Every ambiguity detracts from the value of the sign, and empties it of its meaning. When I pretend something, the sign is actually not there any more, but another sign has replaced what should be there. If we consider this last thesis carefully, we will find it can be established.

A little gift from a child is so charming simply because the child gives himself so uncomplicatedly through his gift, and is totally in it. An expensive wedding gift, on the contrary, with which wealthy and uninterested people express primarily their own status, becomes a poor gift.

SIGN-VALUE AND CREATIVE POWER

The sign-value of a sign depends not only on the veracity, but also on the creative power of the person who gives it. Only people can give signs. Only people can make a physical body subjective to a sign. Signs always belong in the realm of a creative freedom that is capable of conveying meaning.

The first physical body to be made subjective is one's own body. From the very beginning, the body I possess is imbued with undeveloped intentions and meanings. I must develop these personally, in order to be fully at home in my body and in order to make it into the physical entity which is me. Only then can I fully operate my body as a sign: in word and gesture, song and dance. To make one's own body subjective to a sign, one must train not only its motor proficiency, but one must develop, first and foremost, its inner forces in order to give it meaning. This inner strength must be constantly renewed through heart-searching: to make my body become a sign, I must constantly pull myself out of a state of confusion in order really to be present in myself. When I am distracted, my handshake will have little meaning and little sign-power; only when I have returned to myself can I speak to the other personally through my handshake.

The determining factor in creative power comes perhaps more clearly into focus if it is a matter of converting an object outside myself into a sign. Not only is creative imagination needed to discover a good sign—for example, to find a suitable gift—but a great deal of generosity and suggestive power is needed as well, before this sort of sign-activity can be carried into effect. It is just this power to give and convey meaning that determines the degree to which the object is made subjective, and also the degree of one's personal presence in the sign.

THE EFFICACY OF THE SIGNS

The sign becomes reality itself, and an incarnation of life itself, according to its truth-content.

As soon as one has made a division between reality and sign, a number of false problems begin to pile up. The question arises whether a sign can indeed be effective and how a sign can operate. This is actually a false question. The sign can function simply because it is reality itself. The word summons me because my friend's invitation is present in it. The kiss makes love grow because love itself is embodied in it. The gift consolidates our relationship because the attention we pay to one another thus gains a tangible form.

The sign can function because it is reality itself, but it will only be effective according to the degree in which it is understood as a sign. It does not function as something charged with a magic force, but it functions through its meaning, not merely insofar as that meaning is rationally understood, but also as it appears suggestively; not merely as I grasp it with my intellect, but as I sense it with my entire person.[8] The functioning of the sign lies with the word that evokes and with the picture that recalls: not with the forces of physics, nor with magic, but through invitation and freedom.

---

[8] The sign functions also in the direction of its meaning. It functions according to its meaning, *i.e.*, according to the aspect of reality it stands for and which is embodied in it.

DIVERSITY AND GRADATION OF THE SIGNS

A whole gradation of relationships can come to life in different signs.

There is, for instance, the sign of the New Year's card I write to a person with whom I maintain only this form of contact. This card is the sign of my relationship. Weak though it may be, it is the bearer of my relationship, and in it the actual form of my relationship is expressed. When the time comes that I decide to write no more New Year's cards, I feel that I am relinquishing this relationship.

There is also the sign of the meal, the sign of the shared table. This is a copious sign that can exist in many forms: the everyday meal and the Sunday table, the wedding banquet and the farewell dinner. The meal shared by mourners is the expression of the fact that we do not wish to leave the members of the immediate family alone after the funeral. We stay with them for a little while. In joining the group at the table, we affirm our continuing connection with the family.

The conversation and the gift, the song and the dance are still other signs.

Sign-activity has its strongest expression when one is involved in it with one's own body, as in the case of the kiss, by means of which I make my own body into a sign.

Through this sign-activity a relationship can also achieve its fullest development. When a man and woman become totally involved with one another and when their relationship attains form through their living together, a form which is given further meaning through their physical union, this sign can renew their relationship in a radical way by giving life to a new personal sign: the child, the sign of the relationship between this man and this woman. Their relationship is then carried further—it characterizes them as father and mother. The most radical sign is true martyrdom: the sign of the love that remains true, even when the body is broken. Whereas no other sign can ever express total reality (in all its aspects), or completely use up the person, this sign literally exhausts life itself. This death is not to be regarded primarily as a destruction of the human activity, but more explicitly as its completion.

THE MANIFOLD VARIETY OF SIGNS

Life's many forms and the many varieties of relationships can only be expressed adequately in a multitude of signs. Each sign is limited. One single sign never covers a full existence. There must be many signs. If we fail to use a large number of signs, we narrow down both our own existence and our communal existence. The community does not achieve its fullest development.

When we neglect the language of the signs, we become speechless; the result is solitude. The loneliness of modern life has something to do with the fact that the signs through which we could join together have become hollow, we have allowed them to become extinct.

In the world of signs, one sign explains another. Many signs need the verbal sign to elucidate them as a sign and to be fully understood. Whenever several signs function together, they build up a joint situation. The whole situation, in turn, again gives color to the sign-value of each sign functioning in it.

SIGNS AND HISTORY

All great signs have a history: they have a certain meaning from the past, or have gradually acquired a whole gamut of meanings.

Young people in a youth camp can become so solidly bound together through singing a certain song that after a time the whole atmosphere of this gathering is embodied for them in this song. This song takes on a new sound for them, its sign-value increases, and it acquires a history of its own.

Sometimes a gesture can be launched in history by one single person; it can acquire its own meaning for a whole community, originating from one person and his emotion; for example, the V-sign of Churchill during World War II.

In the course of a conversation, two people often find one particular word which takes on an added meaning for them. A sign that functions inside the framework of a

relationship acquires a history of its own within this com-
plicated relationship. To the extent that the relationship
in this sign makes history, the sign also shares in this history: by this means it gains in sign-value. In this way,
many signs have acquired their own sign-value in the
course of the history they have experienced during a particular culture. These signs must also be comprehended
from the point of view of their own history.

The wine-sign has consequently acquired abundant
substance in Jewish history.

Wine is not only the festive drink that gladdens the
heart of man,[9] nor is it preeminently the sign of mascu-
line friendship.[10] It is explicitly the sign of the plenitude
promised by God to his people. In a primary stage, wine
is the sign of the promised land. When Moses sent men
out to explore the land of Canaan and to bring back
some of the fruits of that land, they cut off a branch with
one cluster of grapes on it, in the valley of the Eshcol.
They had to carry these on a stick between two of
them.[11]

Later on, wine becomes the sign of plenty for the Messianic period. The wine-miracle at Cana[12] is the most
powerful illustration of this. Jesus also hinted in this same
connection that the new covenant concluded in his per-

[9] Psalm 104, 15.
[10] Ecclesiastes 9, 10.
[11] Numbers 13, 23.
[12] John 2, 1-11.

son was a new wine that would cause the old bottles to burst.[13]

Lastly, wine is the sign of fulfillment in the last hour. In Matthew and Mark, as well as in Luke, we find Jesus' word: I will not drink henceforth of this fruit of the vine, until that day when I drink it new with you in my Father's Kingdom.[14]

If one wishes to grasp fully the sign-value of the draught of wine in the eucharist, one has to be familiar with this sign's own history. This also applies to the sign of blood.

For the Jews, blood is the sign of life;[15] blood is life itself,[16] the life which only God controls, in such a manner that it may not be utilized by man.[17] Man may only make use of it in order to express his relationship with God. The covenant between God and his people is then concluded and sealed with the blood of sacrificial animals, half of which is sprinkled on the altar which represents Jehovah and the other half on the people.[18] The shed blood has become the sign of the covenant.

In summing up, we can say that signs are the incarnation of reality, and thereby make history. Yet they have

---

[13] Matthew 9, 17.
[14] Matthew 26, 29, Mark 14, 25, Luke 22, 18.
[15] Leviticus 7, 14.
[16] Deuteronomy 2, 23.
[17] Deuteronomy 12, 16.
[18] Exodus 24, 3-8.

their own history. For that reason, the new history which they make is always linked with the history they already have. To be fully familiar with the miraculous world of signs, we must also know their history.

2

Thanking and Remembering

In his wonderful book on the philosophy of Heidegger, Sam. Ijsseling writes: "When man becomes a human being, everything has already begun. The world is already habitable and accessible. Everything he finds around him has already been 'given' . . . Nevertheless, that which has been given is no *fertige Tatsache*, but always and essentially an assignment offered. What is given must be taken up. The thing given is only really given when it is actually received . . . In the fulfillment of the 'assignment' of what is given, the original 'giving' again takes place." [19]

[19] Sam. Ijsseling, *Heidegger, Denken en danken, geven en zijn*, p. 102.

Just as with the fulfilling of the assignment of the gift, declining it or remembering it are two ways of receiving it, and, accordingly, of causing the original giving to take place. They are, therefore, two closely related possibilities for bringing us into contact with the deepest foundations of our human existence.

GIVING OF THANKS

To give thanks is to reveal oneself joyfully to the giver and thus, by receiving, to share in carrying out the giving. If a young man has taken a fancy to a girl and—"still uneasy about speaking"—offers her some flowers, this is an invitation and . . . it *can* remain only that. Only when the girl accepts the flowers gladly can a real relationship exist.

In the gift, the giver includes an appeal for a personal relationship with the one to whom he has offered his gift. The personal relationship between the person giving and the person receiving is achieved through the grateful acceptance of the gift: the personal relationship becomes mutual, and free encounter follows. A gift is only fully a gift if it has been thankfully received.[20] To give thanks is to recognize the gift as a gift and to accept it with one's whole personality.

The peculiar quality of the gift is that it is given freely.

[20] Cf. S. Ijsseling, *op. cit.* p. 98.

One receives it without earning it; the gift is not a reward. It is something gratis, given you as a favor by the other person. It is born of another's generosity, not of a sense of duty and not of a desire to receive thanks. "In the gift one comes into a sphere in which a typical *freedom* is dominant, and indeed, to state it more clearly, not the moral freedom we possess for doing our duty, but a freedom that surpasses this and becomes, as a result, truly a bestowing freedom. Only when I give more than is merited, simply out of the abundance of my heart, do I elevate myself into the sphere of this freedom. And it is also here that the gift acquires its special human value. I am a human being in the full sense of the word only where I can give." [21]

Gratitude is also born of freedom, just as the gift is. Gratitude can never be extorted; when I express thanks I am a free person in relation to the giver. I freely reveal myself to the giver in the joy of my thankfulness. The giving of thanks is my share in consummating freely the gift bestowed on me.[22] Gratitude, therefore, is far more than a social virtue. Humanity stands or falls with gratitude: it is the determining factor in one's own personal attitude to life, where this is seen and understood as a gift freely given.

[21] O. Bollnow, *Nieuwe geborgenheid,* p. 91.
[22] Cf. S. Ijsseling, *op. cit.* Het danken als meevoltrekken van het geven, p. 97.

REMEMBRANCE

Remembering is pausing to think of something originally bestowed and relating it in this way to ourselves. To remember or commemorate is to think of a person or an event from the past, whereby we arrive at what this means for us now. When we remember Pope John or President Kennedy we summon them before us again with our thoughts; we become aware of the truth in what they have done, we lay ourselves open and are ready to continue tracing the line that they have begun. Commemoration is drawing something meaningfully out of the oblivion of the past in order to see it now as a guide to direct us.

Commemoration in its strongest form is thinking of a beginning, of a source, of a happening which in its origin was significant and rich in meaningful impetus. In commemorating, we absorb the original meaning again. Thus we cause the significant person or event to return to our midst in a pertinent way. This causing, through commemoration, of an original significant event to happen again is not mere repetition, for something new is always added; it takes place, for one thing, in a new situation and under new concrete circumstances. The idea of causing an event to recur is best illustrated by the word *revision,* that is, making the original conception topical again, to be experienced here and now.

THANKFUL REMEMBRANCE

Full human remembrance is always thankful remembrance. This is the richest form of receiving something given, of fully converting into a gift something given earlier, of bringing an initial personal relationship back to life now. Thankful remembrance does not merely establish a link with the past, but also determines our attitude in the future: in thankful remembrance I fully accept the assignment contained in the gift.

"It is important to see that within the thinking, the thanking and the remembering, something *happens*. The past is once more drawn out of the obscurity of forgetfulness. Consequently, a future is opened. Through thinking, the events of the past are reenacted; this makes them meaningful here and now, and they acquire significance. The 'giving' from the past turns into a 'coming' in the present. This is a 'happening.' It takes place through thinking. If there is no thinking—that is, thankful remembering,[23] then no 'happening' takes place." [24]

[23] Our note.
[24] S. Ijsseling, *op. cit.* p. 119.

3

Ritual Remembrance among Primitive Peoples

The modern awareness of a gift being only really given when it is received was a vital belief among primitive peoples, for example, in myths and rites.

At one time there existed in Java a ritual that had to be performed when the rice was planted. Sensing that fertility is ultimately a gift and that the planting of rice should be a sacramental event, the Javanese did this in the old original manner, just as described in the myth.

THE MYTH

Man has always been a creature seeking meaning and creating meaning. He wants to see, and especially to experience, the meaning of things. Mankind's first attempt at

31

seeing and experiencing meaning is the myth. Here we are
dealing with a pre-philosophical,[25] yet very rich approach
to the meaning of life. The language spoken in the myth is
never that of sharply defined philosophical conception.
The language of the myth is that of suggestive images and
signs. What this language lacks in clarity it makes up for
in suggestive power; what it lacks in rational delineation
it makes up for by allowing sufficient scope for man's
emotionalism to come into full play.

In the myth, and in the ritual which brings it up to date,
primitive man tries to give meaning to the present and to
make meaning available from the past. The myth always
deals with a meaning belonging to the present. By telling a story from prehistoric times, when life and relationships first came into being, a story gives meaning to present-day life and social living. The myths always tell us
how a particular reality came to exist and how things are
related. They tell us of the origin of matter and spirit, land
and water, man and beast, man and woman, work and
rest, good and evil, war and peace, and also of birth and
death. They reveal the original design of all great realities,
a design that serves as a suggestive model for everything happening now. In this way, relationships and happenings gain their meaning from the original pattern
and from the original event in mythical prehistory.

[25] The myth, among other things, does not have at its disposal the
classified system of concepts that philosophy has.

Primitive man attributes the world's actual existence to the actions of the gods. Since the actions of the gods stem from their abundance of life, their mode of behavior is taken as an example for all worthy actions. Only this particular mode of conduct brings fullness of life. The whole code of behavior among primitive peoples is tied in with the sacred sphere, and therefore only what is sacred or consecrated is completely real to them. Anything that was not done before in prehistoric times by the gods belongs to the sphere of the profane and seems, as such, of little importance in the eyes of primitive man. One only really becomes a human being with the help of divine examples, since only these are creative and, being so, provide meaning. Only those actions of man that are based on a mythical example have meaning and value. Anything done without the mythical prototype is ultimately worthless and unreal for the primitive person.[26] Mythical prehistory is therefore not a closed period of the past, but a period that continues to live in the present. This period of prehistory is the model for all times and for all happenings.[27]

THE REMEMBRANCE RITE

In the remembrance rite of primitive peoples, the event that originally gave meaning to the myth is performed in

[26] Cf. Mircea Eliade, *Het gewijde en het profane,* p. 52.
[27] G. van der Leeuw, *De primitieve mens en de religie,* p. 112.

word and action. This rite of remembrance is always a ceremonial retelling and reenactment of the ancient event. It is never just simple storytelling, but explicitly a ritual narration. It is also not a question of telling something new; it is a solemn narrative of the ancient event that is already familiar to everyone. This story, told in the form of a ritual proclamation, is meant to make one identify oneself with the ancient happening, so that all can join in the enactment of the inspiring event. We might add, incidentally, that this ritual narrative often deals exclusively with particular times and places, and among many primitive peoples it is only the initiated, or the wholly fit fellow tribesmen, who are allowed to be present.

For primitive people the remembrance rite is a commemorative sign-activity, by which the thing commemorated is given the present tense and thereby becomes a new reality for them. The rite is the ancient event brought up to date: this event has now become a sign for them. Its meaning now implicates them, and is accepted and experienced by them.

Should one forget the ancient event narrated in the myth, then every creation comes to nothing, and man leads an unreal, senseless existence. For this reason, an enormous responsibility is tied in with the celebration of rites and with the ritual commemoration of mythical happenings. Primitive man considers himself responsible at two levels: the human level and the cosmic level. He must, in the first place, constantly identify himself again with the ancient event in order to be able to lead a meaningful life, since only the original mythical event really expresses meaning. Besides this, primitive man considers himself responsible at a cosmic level: he deems it necessary to bring the deeds of the gods to life again, in order that the cosmos should remain capable of sanctifying and renewing the world.

MAGIC, OR HUMAN SUGGESTION?

This liturgy of the primitive peoples can seem full of magic to us. It is important, however, to be able to understand it in its own setting, within the framework of primitive man's whole way of life and at his own level of development. When primitive man commemorates the prehistoric happening in a ritual, he ascribes no powers to objects, but wishes to take part in the reenactment of the significant event. It has, therefore, nothing to do with magic, but with a genuine human expression.

Primitive man, however, has little of the individual in his life; his own individuality is weak. Not only is he totally bound up, for better or for worse, with his fellow tribesmen, but he also lives in a cosmic alliance with the natural world surrounding him. He is not yet very conscious of his own subjectivity. It is therefore understandable that he is still not capable of distinguishing, on the one hand, between the moderation of natural laws enacted in the passing of the seasons, in the rising of the

sun and moon, in weather conditions and in the growth
of plants; and, on the other hand, personal expression. Because of this he sometimes attempts to maintain the bal-
ance of natural law by means of his own suggestive rites.
He thinks, for instance, that a certain ritual is needed to
make the sun rise the next day.

We may call this naïve, and of course it is. This naïveté
can be ascribed to a limited capacity for dissociating from
things. Nevertheless, this naïveté must not become a
reason for regarding myth and ritual as magic. Primitive
man's view is that only the consecrated is completely real.
The ritual, by which he commemorates and experiences,
also has nothing magic in it, but has a fundamentally on-
tological character. Primitive man reaches back to what
he regards to be the primal *foundation of the meaning*.

The myth, as a system for explaining the origins of the
world, is simplistic. Yet it is equally simplistic to interpret it primarily in this light. As a way of confronting the
given reality, the remembrance rite (within the framework of mythical belief) still shows great human depth.

In the mythical view and the ritual act of primitive
man, we find the forceful admission that the greatest
things in his existence are given to him; that neither man
nor the world originates from man. The primitive person fully realizes this, and within the framework of this
belief does not shirk his own responsibility: he remains
faithful to the meaning already given him, to the meaning
he thinks he discovers. He is aware of the necessity of a

meaningful existence as his greatest obligation; he regards himself as responsible for the continued existence of the world. He may not forget. He must perform the ritual at fixed times, accurately and punctually, in order to preserve both his own meaningful existence and that of the world.

As we have already mentioned, he is still not capable of dissociating himself spiritually from what has been given. There is still little possibility for personal freedom. The totally obligatory character of the rite bears down upon him as a terrifying duty. His freedom is, as it were, crushed beneath it. Still we must appreciate the fact that the primitive person, in spite of his limited freedom resulting from his own living conditions and his own level of development, does know how to build the remembrance rite functionally into his life: it helps him to exist meaningfully, to bring clarity into his life and to give it perspective.[28]

---

[28] We hope it is clear that we have limited ourselves in this chapter to the main original myths in their simplest form. Naturally many corruptions and magic practices are also found among primitive peoples.

4

The Memorial Meal in Israel

In Israel, also, we find again the pattern of bringing an original inspiring event into the present through commemoration. The original happenings that are commemorated, however, are not happenings from mythical prehistorical times, but are historic events from the history of Israel. The facts behind the founding of the Jewish people are seen as the work of God's hand: these are deeds of salvation, by which God enters their history and puts a history of salvation into motion.

The commemoration of these events is experienced by the Jewish people when they recall them to the present, proclaiming them in such a way that they become accessible now, so that one can partake of them. The cult-proclamation of Jehovah's deeds of salvation is an acceptance and a shared celebration of God's acts of salvation for his people. The commemoration of the great acts of salvation took place among the Jews mainly in the memorial meal: either in the fairly simple Sabbath meal or in the more festive Passover meal.

THE EVENTS IN THE FOUNDING OF THE JEWISH PEOPLE

The exodus from Egypt, the passage through the Red Sea, the covenant on Sinai and the entry into the land of Canaan are the great acts of salvation by which Jehovah gathered the children of Israel together to become his people.

1. The Exodus from Egypt (Exodus 12)

And Jehovah spake unto Moses and Aaron in the land of Egypt: This month shall be for you the beginning of months, the first month of the year. Speak ye unto all the congregation of Israel: On the tenth day of this month every man shall take a lamb for his family, one for every family . . . Ye shall keep it until the fourteenth day of the same month, whereupon the whole assembly of the congregation of Israel shall kill it in the evening. Then they shall take of the blood, and strike it on the two side posts and on the upper door post of the houses, wherein they shall eat it. And they shall eat the flesh in that night, roasted with fire, as well as unleavened bread and bitter herbs. And ye shall eat none of it raw, nor boiled in water; but it must be roasted with fire, head, legs and trunk in one piece. And ye shall also keep none of it until the morning; but shall burn what remains of it with fire until the morning. And thus shall ye eat it: with your loins girded, your shoes on your feet, and your staff in your hand; and ye shall eat it in haste, for it is Jehovah's passover.

For I will pass through the land of Egypt this night, and will smite all the firstborn in Egypt, both man and beast, and against all the gods of Egypt I will execute judgment: I am Jehovah! But the blood shall be the sign upon the houses that ye dwell there; and when I see that blood, I will pass mercifully over you, so that nothing will destroy you when I smite the land of Egypt . . .

Then Moses called for all the elders of Israel, and said unto them: Go,—take the sheep for your families, and kill the passover. Then shall ye take a bunch of hyssop, dip it in the blood that is in the basin, and strike the lintel and the two side posts with blood from the basin: and none of you shall go out of the door of his house until morning. For Jehovah will pass through to smite the Egyptians; but when He seeth the blood upon the lintel and the two side posts, He will mercifully pass by the door, and will prevent the destroyer from entering your houses to smite you . . . And the children of Israel went away and did just as Jehovah had commanded Moses and Aaron.

In the middle of the night Jehovah smote all the first-

born in the land of Egypt, from the firstborn of Pharaoh
that sat on his throne unto the firstborn of the prisoner in
the dungeon; and all the firstborn of cattle. And Pharaoh
rose up and fled in the night with all his court, and all the
Egyptians, and a terrible cry was heard in Egypt; for there
was not a house where there was not one dead. And still
by night he called for Moses and Aaron, and said: Get
ready and depart from among my people; go with the children of Israel to serve Jehovah, as ye have said. Also
take your sheep and your cattle with you, as you have
asked, but be gone; and pray for mercy also for me.
Also the Egyptians urged the people to leave the land
with the greatest haste; for they said: Otherwise we all
shall die! And before the dough was leavened, the people
had to take it with them; their kneading-troughs, wrapped
in their clothes, they carried upon their shoulders . . .
From the dough, which they had brought with them from
Egypt, they had to bake unleavened cakes; for they had
no leavened dough because the Egyptians had driven
them away, without giving them time to prepare food for
the journey . . . It was a night of wakefulness for Jehovah, when He caused them to depart from
Egypt . . .[29]

[29] When reading this story, we must not lose sight of the fact that
this is not a direct account of the historical exodus. It is already
the memorial narrative of the Passover celebration, in which the
historical fact is thankfully commemorated. It is composed of several different liturgical texts.

2. *The Passage through the Red Sea* (*Exodus 14*)

When also the king of Egypt was told that the people had fled, the feelings of Pharaoh and of his court changed toward the people, and they thought: Why have we done this, that we have let Israel go from serving us?

Pharaoh had a good army at his disposal and with this he pursued the unarmed Israelites.

But God took care of his people. When the Egyptians were already in sight, the Israelites discovered a place to cross the water—"Jehovah caused the sea to go back by a strong east wind all that night"—and they fled into Arabia. The pursuing Egyptians were taken unawares crossing the dry patch and they drowned in the sea.

This miraculous escape through the sea marshes was regarded by Israel as the work of God's hand. Through this occurrence, all Jewish history has come to be interpreted as one great heroic deed of Jehovah.

Exodus 14 is made up of two older stories completely interwoven with each other. One story uses forceful mythical language (for example, walls of water that remain standing upright), the other is more suggestive of an accidental conjunction of circumstances (for example, a strong east wind which causes the marshy area to run dry, so that it can be crossed).

The form in which this miracle happens is, however, not so important. What is important is that the believing

Israelite recognizes this miraculous crossing as a sign of God's solicitude for his people.

Myth and history must not be confused with one another. But in this case the language of the myth appeals to us so strongly because it expresses more ornately and more forcefully than any historical account the belief in the God who saves.

3. The Covenant on Sinai (Exodus 19-24)

The covenant that God had made with Abraham was extended on Sinai to include all of the people descended from Abraham, Isaac and Jacob. "Jehovah called to Moses from the mountain: Ye have seen what I did unto the Egyptians, how I bore you on eagles' wings and brought you unto myself. Therefore if ye will obey my voice, and keep my covenant, ye shall be a peculiar treasure unto me above all people; for all the earth is mine. Ye shall be unto me a kingdom of priests and an holy nation." [30]

When Moses has proclaimed the law of Jehovah and the people have accepted this as the way to experience their loyalty to Jehovah, this covenant is sealed with blood:[31] "Then Moses returned to the people and told them all the words and commandments of Jehovah. And all the people answered with one voice: All that

[30] Exodus 19, 3-6.
[31] See above, p. 23.

Jehovah hath said will we do! And Moses wrote all the commandments of Jehovah. The following morning he built an altar at the foot of the mountain and set up twelve pillars according to the number of the twelve tribes of Israel. Then he ordered young men of the children of Israel to offer burnt offerings, and to slaughter young oxen as peace offerings for Jehovah. Then Moses took half of the blood and put it in basins; the other half he sprinkled on the altar. Then he took the book of the covenant and read it in the audience of the people. They said again: All that Jehovah hath said will we do, and be obedient. Now Moses took the blood, sprinkled it on the people, and said: Behold, this is the blood of the covenant which Jehovah hath made with you: it is based on these commands." [32]

4. *The Entry into the Land of Canaan*

We are told in the book of Joshua and also in the liturgical texts of Deuteronomy 6 that Jehovah, true to his promise, led the people into the land of Canaan. And thus they were given a land to live in.

> "Trust in God because of Canaan,
> abundant land of grapes and grain,
> that overflows with milk and honey.
> Yielding its timely harvest ever,

[32] Exodus 24, 3-8.

land of total fruitfulness:
blessed land in which to live!" [33]

GROUND-STRUCTURE OF THE JEWISH MEMORIAL MEAL

In the sacral Jewish memorial meal there are tradi-
tionally two religious mealtime rituals that express what
this meal as a whole is intended to be: the blessing with
the breaking of bread at the beginning of the meal, and
then a similar but more solemn ritual at the end of the
meal—the thanksgiving toast with wine. Between the
two thanksgiving rituals, the real meal was eaten. The
opening ritual (the breaking of bread) consisted of four
stages:

1. The chairman of the group at table took the bread
in his right hand and held it just above the table.

2. He gave a thanksgiving prayer, praising Jehovah
for the gifts he gives.

3. He broke the bread.

4. And lastly, he distributed it to all present at the
table; they all ate some of the bread to confirm his thanksgiving prayer.

The closing ritual (the toast with wine) consisted of
three stages:

1. The chairman of the group at table took the goblet
of wine in his right hand and held it just above the table.

[33] T. Naastepad, Een lied om Kanaän.

2. Then he gave a thanksgiving prayer, praising Jehovah for the great things he had done for his people in creation and covenant.

3. Lastly, they all confirmed his thanksgiving prayer by drinking with him from their own goblets.

We can more or less compare this closing ritual of the wine-toast with our own toasting ritual at a reception or banquet table: by joining the chairman in drinking, we confirm the words he has spoken and ritually partake in his address.

THE FEAST OF THE PASSOVER

The most important memorial meal known to the Jews was the feast of the Passover.

Before the breaking of bread and before the meal itself, there was a ceremonial narration of the history of the flight out of Egypt, the story of Exodus 12. The symbolism of this meal was explained: the particular character of this Passover-night,[34] the paschal lamb, the unleavened bread and the bitter herbs. During the numerous blessings[35] spoken over the foods, the name of Jehovah was gratefully praised for the great miracles he had performed for his people: for the exodus from Egypt and

---

[34] Exodus 12, 42.
[35] There were four goblets, the third of which was the goblet of benediction.

the passage through the Red Sea, for bread and wine, for creation and covenant.

Thankful remembrance was experienced also by the Jews as a participation in the celebration of what Jehovah had given them. The idea of something having-been-given was for them only real when this had been commemorated with thanks.[36] With their grateful commemoration of the exodus and of the passage, they experienced a liberation and a deliverance which took place in the present.[37]

[36] Cf. Sam. Ijsseling, *op. cit.* p. 109.
[37] *Ibid.*

5

Jesus of Nazareth

Wherever man tries to live meaningfully, Jesus becomes the self-constituted original symbol of humaneness. He comes to tell and to demonstrate what it means to exist as a human being: "I am the way, the truth, and the life." [38] In his person we have a model for all human life, a model that holds good for all times: "Before Abraham was, I am." [39]

JESUS IS THE SIGN OF GOD FOR US

In John we read: "Beloved, let us love one another: for

[38] John 14, 6.
[39] John 9, 58.

love is of God; and everyone that loveth is born of God,
and knoweth God. He that loveth not, knoweth not God;
for God is love. In this was manifested the love of God
toward us, because that God sent his only begotten Son
into the world, that we might live through him." [40]

In scripture and tradition Christ is named as the Son
of God become human for our sake. The Father com-
municates himself most forcibly through the Son. Jesus is
God's gift to us of himself in human form. He is also called
God's Word become flesh for us. The person expresses
himself and shares his life through the word. Through
Jesus, God speaks to us in a human way.

In Paul we read that God's love of mankind has become visible in Jesus of Nazareth.[41] He is the sign of the
loving God in our midst. We can see God at work in Jesus;
in this man the divine, or love, becomes visible.

Jesus experienced love for his fellow man in such a
radical way that he brought about a whole revolution in
the Jewish world of that time, a revolution both social
and religious. He broke through all sorts of social barriers.
He comes in contact with Samaritans and heathens. He
helps people on the Sabbath; he does not avoid evil people; he occupies himself with public sinners.

He moves about everywhere, doing good works. He
speaks inspiring words and brings healing. He is gentle in

---

[40] 1 John 4, 7-9.
[41] Cf. Titus 3, 4.

his personal dealings and is concerned for everyone, even for those of least importance. He declares that he has not come to be served, but to serve,[42] and has come expressly to seek that which has been lost.[43]

Both in word and deed, Jesus proclaimed love of mankind; he preached it and demonstrated it through living it.

JESUS THE RELIGIOUS MAN

Jesus leads a life of surrender to his fellow men. In this way he reveals love. Yet he does this in and from a total alliance with God, his and our Father. "He that hath seen me hath seen the Father . . . The words that I speak unto you I speak not of myself; but the Father that dwelleth in me, he doeth the works. Believe me: I am in the Father, and the Father in me." [44] His love for his fellow men, experienced from his alliance with the Father, is his essential form of religiousness; that is, his cult.

This alliance with the Father is defined in the Bible with two words: obedience and faith.

Obedience is performing the bidding of. Jesus received from his Father the assignment of making love visible among men. A free man, he wholly accepted this call, this

[42] Cf. Mark 10, 45.
[43] Cf. Luke 19, 10.
[44] John 14, 9-11.

assignment. He did his Father's bidding. He says that do-ing the will of his Father is his meat:[45] it is his food; he lives from it. To be religious is to love people in a spirit of free obedience to the Father.

Faith. Jesus can give himself to his fellow men because he is secure in his total trust in the Father. "Therefore take no thought, saying, What shall we eat? or, What shall we drink? or, Wherewithal shall we be clothed? For after all these things do the Gentiles seek: for your heavenly Father knoweth that ye have need of all these things. But seek ye first the kingdom of God, and his righteousness; and all these things shall be added unto you. Take therefore no thought for the morrow." [46] To be religious is to give oneself to one's fellow men, fully trusting in the Father, in full confidence that it is right.

Jesus demonstrated this religiosity to mankind by his life. He loved them within and from his alliance with the Father, obedient to and trusting in the Father.

THE GREAT REVELATION OF JESUS' DEATH

Jesus' surrender to mankind and to his Father, his servitude both to God and to mankind, are most strongly expressed in his death. His death is the moment when he appears most forcefully as a gift. With his

[45] Cf. John 4, 34.
[46] Matthew 6, 31-34a.

death he becomes totally a given man: "Therefore doth my Father love me, because I lay down my life, that I might take it again. No man taketh it from me, but I lay it down of myself. I have power to lay it down, and I have power to take it again. This commandment have I received of my Father." [47]

In trusting obedience to his Father, he has remained true to his mission: to make himself into a gift to mankind. He has given himself for his Church,[48] and in doing so has made himself obedient unto death, even the death on the cross.[49] He has remained true in his love to the end, even when his body was broken.

Here, in Jesus, we see what sacrifice really is: not a seeking of suffering and death, but a keeping faith with love, in spite of suffering, to the death. Jesus does not seek suffering. On the contrary, his attitude to suffering and death is one of aversion. We read in the stories of the passion that Jesus was sorrowful and frightened, and prayed to his Father that this cup might pass from him.[50] On the other hand, Jesus comes to a total acceptance of suffering. "This is the cup which my Father hath given me, shall I not drink it?" [51] Jesus remains faithful in his love,

[47] John 10, 17-18.
[48] Cf. Ephesians 5, 25.
[49] Cf. Philippians 2, 8.
[50] See, among others, Mark 14, 34-36.
[51] John 18, 11.

even though this must end in the most negative of experiences. And so his love assumes the form of a sacrifice. The sacrifice that Jesus offers to the Father is not his suffering, as such, but it is his love which fully reveals its strength and faith, in and through suffering. Jesus' sacrifice is his faithful love, which gives way neither to suffering nor to death.

The suffering and death of Jesus are not supposed to reconcile God with mankind, or to make God, as it were, feel well-disposed again toward mankind. If this were the case, God would be a sort of avenging god who demands suffering as a rehabilitation for his own satisfaction. The suffering and death of Jesus are not to reconcile God with mankind, but rather to reconcile mankind with God, so that mankind should accept God—God who reveals himself in the most radical way through Jesus as a God of love.

Jesus' death is a death of revelation. It reveals what love actually is: a giving-up of oneself even unto death. "Greater love hath no man than this, that a man lay down his life for his friends." [52]

Through Jesus' death, God wishes to reconcile mankind with himself, with love. This revelational death serves to make men accessible to, and in possession of, their most profound potentiality—that is, to exist for one another, full of love, as children of one Father. Wherever this great

---

[52] John 15, 13.

sign of Jesus' death is comprehended and accepted, it signifies redemption for man. With his death, a new covenant is made between God and his people.

Jesus' death is also a way to the glory of a fully living resurrection. By laying down his life for love, Jesus conquered the death of lovelessness. He abolished death and brought life to light.[53]

"Therefore let all the house of Israel know assuredly, that God hath made that same Jesus, whom ye have crucified, both Lord and Christ." [54] For his loving obedience "God also hath highly exalted him, and given him a name which is above every name." [55]

Through Jesus' resurrection, the Father confirms that the giving of oneself even unto death was good; and that, through this, Jesus became Lord of all: the exemplary goal which mankind must strive to attain, so that the God of love shall reign supreme in all.

[53] Cf. 2 Timothy 1, 10.
[54] Acts 2, 36.
[55] Philippians 2, 9.

6

The Eucharist of Christ

Jesus celebrated his eucharist in the framework of a Jewish commemoration meal, probably in the more specific form of the Passover meal. We know, moreover, that the meal of the Last Supper was preceded by the ritual of the washing of feet, with which he specifically represents himself as a servant.

Jesus inserts his own thanksgiving into this traditional Jewish framework of the commemoration meal; this thanksgiving acquires an entirely new Christian content.

Jesus thanks his Father for the acts of salvation that the Father has carried out during his life, for those of the past and those yet to come. It is an expression of gratitude for his whole existence in all its aspects: a thanksgiving for his existence as the revelation of God's love of mankind and a thanksgiving for his intimacy, so full of trust, with the Father.

In his prayer of thanks, Jesus proclaims his death as a sign of total surrender. He gives thanks to God that the kingdom is now fully come through him, by his death and resurrection. He gives thanks to God that through his life and death he reveals to mankind that what really matter most in life are love and loyalty, faith and surrender. It is no longer merely a thanksgiving for the food with which Jehovah nourishes his people, but a thanksgiving for the nourishment that gives him life: of doing the will of the Father by appearing, filled with love, among his fellow men. It is no longer merely thanksgiving for the escape from servitude in Egypt, for the passage through the Red Sea and for the entry into the promised land of Canaan, but thanksgiving for his own departure from a world without love, his passage through a revelational death, and his entry into the kingdom of love, into the glory of the Father.

No longer is it an offering of thanks for the old covenant, but for the new Testament in his blood.

In the thanksgiving prayer that he offered with the bread, and with the breaking and sharing of the bread, Jesus must have made the surrender of his life so self-evident and clear that his disciples understood he was giving himself wholly to them in offering them bread of thanksgiving, for Luke is able to record of this: "This is my body which is *given* for you." [56] And likewise, in uttering thanks over the chalice and in passing it around, he must have explained the surrender of his life with such clarity that his disciples understood he was giving himself totally to them and to all mankind in the chalice of benediction, so that this could be reported as "This is my blood . . . which is shed for many." [57] He must have made it clear that this giving of himself meant redemption for mankind so that Matthew[58] can speak of "the blood of the new testament, which is shed for the remission of sins." [59] In this whole ritual event, he made his life's surrender so topical that the Church has always believed he brought into this rite the very same sacrifice of life that was to be carried out the next day in his suffering and dying.

When Jesus takes up bread and wine to give thanks in this manner to his Father for the redemption of all men, a redemption which he consummates by surrendering his life, then both that surrender and the redemption become actuality.

When he gives thanks that the supremacy of love is manifested through his surrender of life, he fully acknowledges in this thanksgiving that he is a man given. The giving of thanks is always a component of the having-

---

[56] Luke 22, 19.
[57] Mark 14, 24.
[58] Matthew 26, 28.
[59] Cf. F. Hofmans, TvL 1961; 69-70.

been-given.[60] The characteristic form of Jesus' celebration of the eucharist during the Last Supper is a memorial meal in which he expresses thanks for having been totally given. In this meal he gives thanks for his revelational life-sacrifice and consummates this sacrifice in thanksgiving.[61] Jesus' eucharist is not just a reference to the sacrifice which will follow, but is already this sacrifice in a sign-activity. It is a sign-activity which, in the profoundest sense of the word, comprises a real and actual surrender of life.

Jesus' thanksgiving is the ritual celebration of his Passover, of his passage out through suffering and death to resurrection. It is the ritual celebration of the New Testament which will then be sealed in his blood. It represents the suffering and death which precede the resurrection. The sealing in his blood—the sign of life—which is shed for all, shows that the offering, made by him in thankfulness, is a covenantal sacrifice.[62]

Where bread and wine are included in the sign-activity through which Jesus gratefully gives himself, the eating of this bread and the drinking of this wine mean a com-

---

[60] Cf. S. Ijsseling, *op. cit.* p. 98.

[61] With this, we can again confirm that, with Christianity, the offering or sacrifice must not be seen as linked with the sacrifices of the heathens and Jews, but rather in connection with the general trend of "blessing—thanksgiving—thank-offering" of the Old Testament. Cf. F. Hofmans, *op. cit.* p. 72.

[62] Cf. *supra* pp. 44-45.

munion with the self-giving Christ. When the disciples, giving their thanks with Jesus, eat of this bread and drink from the chalice, they too receive, acknowledge and proclaim his love as the greatest in their life, and they join into the new covenant of God with his people.

With this a number of aspects of this rich sign of Jesus' eucharist are shown: included in the Jewish memorial meal, it is a prayer of thanks in which he proclaims his death through prayer; ritually makes his Passover present; celebrates the new covenant, and gathers his disciples together in the sign of unity.

7

The Eucharist of the Church

MEANING

With the words "This do in remembrance of me," [63] Jesus gave his Church the assignment of commemorating his death and resurrection in order to perpetuate through the ages his revealing and redeeming death on the cross.[64] His disciples accepted this assignment of celebrating in this way all he means for us, until he returns and until God's love shall reign supreme.

In conjunction with the eucharist of the Lord Jesus, the Church thankfully remembers his life, his death and his resurrection. It thereby shares all the aspects of Jesus'

[63] Luke 22, 19 and 1 Corinthians 11, 24-25.
[64] Cf. *Constitutie over de heilige liturgie,* nr. 47.

eucharist, which it takes up and assimilates according to its own situation. It is no longer merely the offering of Christ, but also the offering of the Church. It is an offering of the whole Christ, in which we are actively absorbed and in which we take part through our belief in Christ —that is to say, through our personal surrender. Consequently, the Eucharist of the Church is:

1. The proclamation of Jesus' meaningful attitude to life and of the revelation of his death: "For as often as ye do this, ye do show the Lord's death." [65]

Jesus' meaningful attitude to life, most strongly expressed in His sacrificial death, is acknowledged and followed by us. In thankful remembrance we accept the task which his example sets for us.

2. The renewal of revision of the new covenant: "The celebration of the eucharist is the meeting of God with his people, in the covenanted sacrifice of his Son, our Lord and brother." [66] As such, it is the sacrament that brings the Church together, the sign of the unity of all believers, and the indication of the possibility for the deepest communion among men.

3. The "Viaticum," the provisions for the Church on its pilgrimage to the celestial Jerusalem. The eucharist celebration aims to bring a people out of an existence purely within the world into the new land of the freedom of the children of God.

[65] 1 Corinthians 11, 26.
[66] Pastoral letter of the Netherlands Episcopacy on the Eucharist, Utrecht, April 27, 1965.

It is therefore directed toward the future, and is ultimately a promise and a guarantee of his return.

DEVELOPMENT

The celebration of the eucharist has undergone evolution through the centuries. What Jesus actually did during the Last Supper is no longer so easily recognizable in the structure of the Mass as we know it today. The rich sign of the Last Supper has become, on the one hand, somewhat shrunken in several of its aspects, and yet on the other hand, new elements have been added to it.

1. Diminishing of the Memorial Meal

The prayers of thanksgiving over the bread and wine, both constituent rituals of the Jewish memorial meal, had already acquired a certain independence in the Last Supper. Jesus gave to his thanksgiving a new content, by which this thank-offering acquired a meaning beyond that of the Jewish memorial meal. His instruction "this do in remembrance of me" [67] also refers only to these particular thanksgiving rites.

During the apostolic period, the two thank-offerings were brought together and put at the end of the meal as one ritual whole. This is already reflected in the narratives of Matthew and Mark.

Later, these novel eucharistic rites were detached from

the meal. A double development was launched with this separation of agape and eucharist:

a. The emphasis comes to be placed more upon the prayer of thanks, less on the consumption of the food, and, as time goes on, on the consumption of the eucharistic foods. Subsequent influences of an entirely different sort, such as the crusade against Arianism when Christ's divinity was one-sidedly stressed, will cause the communion to be almost totally omitted.

b. The omission of the meal also led to the result that one no longer saw the essence of the former memorial meal so clearly, i.e. the *thankful remembrance* which explicitly comprised the character of the sacrifice. It is therefore understandable that later theologians occasionally went astray in elaborating on the sacrificial character of the eucharist, seeking their inspiration in the pattern of heathen sacrifices.

2. Insertion of the Verbal Service

As Jews, the early Christians remained faithful to the synagogue service: before they celebrated the eucharist in any house, they visited the temple for the Jewish reading and prayer service: "And they, continuing daily with one accord in the temple, and breaking bread from house to house, did eat their meat with gladness and singleness of heart." [68]

Partly because of the admission of non-Jewish Chris-

[68] Acts 2, 46.

tians, and partly because of the Jewish tradition that verbal proclamation and sacrifice belong together (the covenant proclaimed verbally must, according to Jewish tradition, always be sanctioned by an offering), the visit to the synagogue was already being omitted at an early date; the reading and prayer service comes to take its own place in the eucharist celebration. This reached its full development between the third and fourth centuries.

The verbal service is organically built into the celebration of the eucharist: one first listens to the word of God and takes it in while praying; this dialogue becomes absorbed into the eucharist ritual. The union of the verbal service and the eucharist service is achieved structurally through the prayer of the believers: this prayer-response made by the believers to the proclamation leads directly to the eucharist prayer of thanks.

In the old Roman liturgy, as well as in many other liturgies, there was a great deal of variation, both in the choice of text and in the duration of the reading. "Read from the Scripture as long as the time permits it." [69] Where this tradition of variation had generally gone out of use, it was restored, to a certain degree, by the Second Vatican Council.

3. Curtailment of the Thanksgiving

For many centuries, the speaker gave the eucharistic thanksgiving in one single impromptu prayer address.

[69] Justinus 1ste Apologie, 67.

Justin indicates clearly that the eucharist must be a long prayer, freely formulated: the speaker must express thanks "as well as he can." [70]

The celebrant improvised this prayer of thanksgiving around several main themes (see, for example, the Traditio apostolica of Hyppolytus, from the second century). This same freedom can often still be found as late as the sixth century in Rome, and the eighth century in Spain.[71]

From the fourth century onward, the free expression of thanksgiving gives way to a set prayer: the canon. This is the beginning of a development through which the prayer of thanks gradually yields ground to prayers that put more emphasis upon the sacrificial aspect, or intercessional prayers (mementos, nobis quoque, etc.).

It is interesting to note that in the new concelebrated Mass these prayers are given less emphasis, since they are uttered neither by the main officiating priest, nor by all the celebrants together.

4. Diminishing of the Liturgy's Popular Character

In the sixth and seventh centuries, the imperial court style made its entry into the liturgy. The whole ceremonial of homages paid to the celebrant creates, therefore, a cleavage between celebrant and people. The appearance

[70] Apol. 65, 3 and 76, 5.
[71] Jungman, *Missarum Solemnia,* 40.

of a choir, playing an increasingly independent role, transforms the ordinary believer into an observer. Popular forms of participation, such as the litany, were omitted or shortened. After the eighth century, the communal character of the liturgy was further threatened by the introduction of a number of individual prayers by the priest, such as the offertory prayers and the prayers preparatory to the celebration of communion.

The retention of Latin in transferring the Roman liturgy to non-Latin areas and the introduction of the custom of no longer uttering the canon as a vocal proclamation further contributed to the alienation of the liturgy from the people. The rigid liturgical form, brought about by the Council of Trent and propagated by the strictly rubrical missal of Pius V, intensified the estrangement between the official liturgy and the living people. The predominantly rubrical character of the liturgical training of priests perpetuated this alienation. The liturgical constitution of the Second Vatican Council is a fundamental improvement.

5. *Infiltration of Distorted Ideas and Practices*

As soon as we lose sight of the context of the thank-offering (sacrifice, implied in the giving of thanks), room is left for all kinds of distorted mystical interpretations. Under their influence, the indoctrinating stories and prayers which belong with the memorial ritual give way to the silent recital of the canon. The proclamation of belief is silenced, whereas it should have found its most expressive form in the eucharistic thank-offering.

The increasing lack of understanding concerning the actual scope of the eucharist and, on the other hand, the people's need to take part in it in some way, have brought many words, gestures and allegorical interpretations into the Mass since the twelfth century. These words and gestures have transformed the Mass into a dramatic spectacle of the suffering of Christ: slipping of the paten under the corporal (Christ concealing himself because his hour is not yet come), the five signs of the cross at the *Unde et memores* (the five wounds of the dying Christ), the bowing of the head after the *memento mori* (the death of Jesus), the raising of the voice at the *nobis quoque peccatoribus* (to suggest the cry of the centurion) and so forth.

From the eighth century, an important shift in the interpretation and experience of the eucharist takes place —a shift from a dynamic to a static interpretation. Instead of being seen as Christ's act of offering himself to the Father, an action in which the people take part, the eucharist is now viewed as a gift of God, which descends from heaven, as it were, with the consecration. Only the celebrant is active; everything is wrapped as much as possible in a mysterious silence.

Up to and including the twelfth century, the communion still came under the sign of bread and wine in general. Then came the scholastic theologians, who directed

their attention to what they called the essence of things
to such an extent that they became blind to the abundance
of signs. As soon as it became evident to them that Christ
gives himself totally in the breaking of the bread, and
that the effectiveness of the communion was thus established in the bread-sign alone, they declared that the dis-
appearance of the chalice constituted no essential loss of
grace. With that, and because of the practical difficulties
involved, the communion under the sign of the wine very
swiftly became a thing of the past. In this way, also, the
specific aspects of the eucharist which were particularly
significant and evocative for this sign were robbed of
their meaning: the festive character of the gathering which
is so spontaneously expressed in the wine-draught, the
sign of the abundance of the messianic period, the reference to the return of the Lord and the contractual character of celebration of the eucharist—all these fell into
the background.[72] For the full experience of the eucharist, it is of far-reaching importance that the Second Vatican Council has reinstated the communion under the sign
of the wine.

[72] See *supra* pp. 22-23.

8

The Actual Presence of Christ

in the Eucharist

In the eucharist Jesus is present for his Church with everything he signifies for it: as the guide in life who reveals in the sacrifice of his own life the essence of true humanity and genuine devotion; as the mediator who revises the alliance of God with his people.

The presence of the Lord Jesus in the bounties of bread and wine is by no means the only form in which he is present in the celebration of the eucharist. He is in evidence there in many forms and it is important to see that these are not detached from one another.

FORMS IN WHICH THE LORD IS ACTUALLY PRESENT

1. The Presence in the Sign of the Community

Since celebration of the eucharist is most expressly a gathering of Christians in the name of the Lord, he is present in the entire assembly celebrating the eucharist. Here the word of the scripture comes explicitly into force: "For where two or more are gathered together in my name, there am I in the midst of them." [73]

2. The Presence in the Sign of the Official Function

The Lord Jesus is present in a special way in those who function as ministers in the celebration of the eucharist. The community celebrating the eucharist is a hierarchically constructed community: the ministers are taken from among the people and are appointed for the people for the benefit of their relationship with God, to offer gifts and sacrifices . . .[74] The Lord has laid his hand upon them in a special way, to reveal himself as high priest through them.

3. Presence in the Sign of the Word

Wherever the word of the Lord is preached, he himself is speaking in our midst.[75] He is present in the speech of the proclaimer. He is present in the congregation which

[73] Matthew 18, 20.
[74] Cf. Hebrews 5, 1.
[75] See *supra* p. 8.

listens and receives his spirit in order to comprehend what he has said.

4. Presence in the Signs of the Eucharist

The Lord Jesus is again present in a special way in the action of the eucharist, in the whole idea of thankful commemoration of his life, death and resurrection, with all that this implies. Wherever bread and wine are included in this sign-activity of thankful remembrance, the Lord is wholly present in person in these signs.

It is important that we should experience dynamically this presence of the Lord in the community and in the signs, and this in a double sense.

a. It is a *happening*. This happening takes place only insofar as the Church is present in a spirit of thankfulness. "The presence streams forth from Christ as boundlessly as his love, but does not achieve its plenitude when we do not believe." [76] Belief in the Church is always essential for the sacramental sign. [77]

b. It is also explicitly a *church-forming* happening. "In our present-day experience, it emerges more clearly that the Lord is present in the gifts of the eucharist in order to be utilized and, by this means, in order to unite us

---

[76] Schoonenberg, quoted in *Katholiek archief,* May 28-June 4, 1965, pp. 636-637.
[77] Cf. E. Schillebeeckx, *Christus, sacrament van de Godsontmoeting,* p. 90.

more closely with him and with each other." [78] The whole structure of the actualized and real presence of the Lord's body in the sign of bread is intended to make him more present in the assembled congregation and in each of its members. The presence which has acquired form is not the final goal of life, but a means of achieving it." [79]

THE MANNER IN WHICH THE LORD IS ACTUALLY PRESENT IN THE SIGNS OF THE EUCHARIST

The Church has always believed that the Lord Jesus is present in the gifts of bread and wine. However, lately there has been some discussion within the Church about "how one can approach and define this mystery of the faith, and how one can try to achieve a closer representation of this true presence."

The fact that this question has been posed is not in itself a symptom of disbelief, but is in the first place a sign that we are concerned with the crux of the matter, that we do not pass it by in a spirit of indifference, that the mystery is still giving rise to thought. If the mystery again sets us thinking, then we can assume that it will go on providing nourishment to life.

The Dutch bishops, in their letter of April 27, 1965,

[78] Pastoral letter of the Netherlands Episcopacy on the Eucharist, Utrecht, April 27, 1965.
[79] Schoonenberg, quoted in *Katholiek archief,* May 28-June 4, 1965, 627.

wrote the following: "We feel that this inquiry into the manner by which Christ becomes present can be left to the theologians for free discussion, so long as the transformation of bread and wine into the body and blood of the Lord is accepted, as well as the truth of his presence in the eucharistic forms. At the same time, however, we urge all those who are occupied with this matter to maintain a devout respect, and show the wisdom of caution in handling the Church's articles of belief." [80]

The answer to the question concerning the manner in which Christ is present will assuredly never be satisfactorily expressed in words. It will perhaps always defy formulation, since both the incarnation and the resurrection of the Lord Jesus and the sending of the spirit to his Church remain for us ineffable secrets: it is impossible for us to penetrate or surmise the divine depths of the subjectivity of Jesus' incarnation, first in human, then in resurrected form; nor will we ever understand how the spirit achieves its creative sovereignty in the Church.

Yet, following our own line of approach, which is only an approximation, we will attempt to draw attention to several points of departure which might be used in considering this question.

1. Consideration from the Point of View of Sign-Activity

The person from whom each sign-activity originates makes himself present in the form of a personal address,

---

[80] Cf. the same Pastoral letter of the Netherlands Episcopacy.

in order to make a relationship with someone else real. When objects are included in this sign-activity, they then become the main body of the person from whom the sign-activity originates; they become an extension of his physical being, through which he comes to life. He is not spatially condensed in them, but they become an embodiment of his personal presence. These objects are totally imbued with the meaning of the whole sign-activity.

It is therefore understandable that the eucharistic bread, within the framework of the whole sign-activity of the breaking of bread, should be wholly imbued with the meaning of this sign-activity, and also with the meaning of Jesus' eucharist celebration, that is to say, of offering himself in gratefulness. The bread is wholly leavened with Christ's giving himself. The reality of his life permeates it, in such a way that we can say that this bread, as well as the wine, is itself the body of the Lord.

Within the total sign-activity of the eucharist, this bread becomes the Lord's body, and due to this activity it remains so. This last concept is comprehensible if we compare it with human gift-giving. Inside the framework of the giving of a gift, my gift becomes the sign of my attention and friendship; it becomes this and it remains this, as long as this gift for my friend exists.

The sign gains its sign-value in proportion to the veracity of the person who presents the sign: he is present in his sign according to the degree of his own truthfulness. We believe that the Lord Jesus had no deceit in him, that he is the true man in every respect and therefore the one who, more than anyone else, is capable of operating the sign and of being present in his signs. We have also already emphasized that the value of the sign-activity, and the degree of personal representation in the signs included in this activity, depend upon the creative power of the person from whom this sign-activity originates. The person's creative power establishes his identity with that of his signs. We believe that the Lord Jesus has incomparable creative powers at his command: "He is the image of the invisible God, the firstborn of every creature. For him were all things created, by him and for him: he is before all things, and by him all things consist." [81] We believe that the radical powers of giving and of inspiring which Jesus possessed make it possible for him to make the bread and wine of the eucharist completely subjective to his body.

Within the whole sign-activity of the eucharist action, the bread and the wine are totally taken up and become relatival. They are brought into relation with the sign-activity as a whole, in order to become a genuine sign of the Lord who gives himself, and in order to become the body which is given up for us, and the blood which is shed for us.

Seen from a purely natural and worldly standpoint, the bread and wine also remain completely themselves.

[81] Colossians 1, 15-17.

"Everything that is inherent to bread and wine remains, but this is included in its entirety in a higher sphere of existence. It is also true here that grace does not destroy the worldly values, but actually has need of them." [82] The eucharist sign-activity in which the bread and the wine acquire an entirely new meaning also demands that the bread and the wine continue to exist on their original level of meaning. This original meaning, developed historically, always contributes something toward clarifying the whole of the sign-activity. It emphasizes that the Lord Jesus' attitude to life is really nourishment for man. It makes us feel that the meaningfulness of Jesus' life should be received with gratitude, in the same way that the eating of the bread and the drinking from the cup during the Jewish Passover functioned as an affirmation of the prayer of thanks offered by the speaker. It causes us to realize that the eucharist gathering is a festive gathering. It keeps alive the expectancy of Jesus' return.

When we say that the bread and wine change into the body and blood of Christ, we mean that we are concerned here with a real metamorphosis, and more explicitly, with the profoundest change that can exist. Still we must try to represent as precisely as possible this change of being. It does not comprise any annihilation of what was already there (the innate character of the bread and wine re-

---

[82] Smits, *Voordracht te Leuven.*

mains), but it does comprise an augmentation of what already existed (the bread becomes far more than it originally was). This metamorphosis of the bread and wine does not lie on the physical level, but is a great deal more fundamental: it is a metamorphosis brought about by a change in meaning, by an increase in meaning. It is a metamorphosis caused by the acquisition of a new significance that integrates the former one and at the same time totally surpasses it.

To say that the bread remains "simply bread" is also completely wrong. Through being absorbed into the sign-activity which increases its significance, it becomes a great deal more than that, and something essentially different from ordinary bread. It still remains wholly bread, yet it becomes something completely different: the body of Christ, surrendered for our sake and become new bread for the believer.

A continual tendency toward naturalistic thinking makes it sometimes difficult to see such a change in meaning as the profoundest metamorphosis. We easily forget that natural phenomena are only brought fully into being by the meaning-giving person. The real creations, however, take place on the level of meaningful freedom; they belong with the person and his word. "In the beginning was the Word, and the Word was with God, and the Word was God. The same was in the beginning with God. All things were made by the Word; and without the Word was not anything made that was made. In the Word was life. . . ." [83] Through his own free sign-activity, into which the person absorbs them, the physical phenomena gain meaning. The person, due to his creative power, can also add new meanings to them. Subsequently, neither the things of nature as such, nor the meanings they have already acquired through history, need to be eliminated.

2. Further Clarification of Thankful Remembrance

Every true human remembrance (thankful remembrance) of a person or of an event makes this person or event present for us with everything it now means to us. With thankful remembrance something really happens.[84] This is even more self-evident when the person whom we are remembering has given us the assignment of remembering him, and has also supplied us with a particular sign-activity with which to do this.

In giving thanks during the Last Supper, Jesus wholly gives himself, and he provides this gift with a visible form by passing round the thanksgiving bread and the cup of blessing.

With its grateful commemoration, the Church piously opens itself to receive this gift, and in so doing, allows Jesus' thankful giving of himself to occur again. In this way, Jesus' act of giving himself in the given bread really

[83] John, from the prologue to his gospel.
[84] See *supra* p. 29.

happens again. This actuality of the happening achieves its full depth for the believer because of the fact that the Lord Jesus is resurrected and lives now. It achieves its full force from the Spirit which constantly reveals through the Church all that the Lord Jesus means to the Church.

Summing up, we can say that in the eucharist we are concerned with the presence of the resurrected Christ, by means of the sign-activity of thankful remembrance. The transformation of the bread and wine into the body and blood of the Lord represents an increase in meaning, brought about by its total subjection in this ecclesiastical sign-activity. By this method of approach, we hope to have eliminated a number of less fortunate interpretations of the mystery, so that this may lead to a clearer conception of the mystery of life, in which Jesus, by breaking the bread and blessing the cup, gives himself totally to the Father and to mankind.

The fact that we wish to clarify the sacramental sign and make it comprehensible does not mean we are eliminating the mystery itself. On the contrary, we are hereby restoring the sign to its proper function, which is that of bringing the mystery to us in the fullness of its appellant force. For the mystery, in the Christian sense, consists of God's acts for the salvation of mankind, made *visible*.